Title of the Book

"The Data-Driven Leader: Empowering Business and Government through Informed Decisions"

By
Ms. Manpreet Kaur
Assistant-Professor
Chandigarh University,
Gharuan, Mohali

Table of Contents

Introduction

- Overview of data-driven leadership
- The importance of informed decision-making in business and government
- Goals and structure of the book

Chapter 1: The Role of Data in Leadership

- Defining data-driven leadership
- The impact of data on decision-making processes
- Case studies of successful data-driven leaders

Chapter 2: Understanding Data Types and Sources

- Types of data: quantitative vs. qualitative, structured vs. unstructured
- Data sources: internal vs. external, primary vs. secondary
- How leaders can identify relevant data for their decision-making needs

Chapter 3: Building a Data-Driven Culture

- Fostering a culture that values data
- Leadership's role in promoting data literacy across teams
- Strategies for encouraging collaboration around data

Chapter 4: Tools and Technologies for Data-Driven Leadership

- Overview of data analysis and visualization tools
- Emerging technologies: AI, machine learning, and big data
- Choosing the right tools for your organization

Chapter 5: Data Collection and Management Strategies

- Best practices for effective data collection
- Data governance: policies and frameworks
- Ensuring data quality and integrity

Chapter 6: Analyzing Data for Informed Decision-Making

- Descriptive, diagnostic, predictive, and prescriptive analysis
- Techniques and methodologies for effective data analysis
- Real-world examples of data analysis driving decisions

Chapter 7: Ethical Considerations and Data Governance

- Importance of ethical data use
- Privacy concerns and regulatory compliance
- Building trust through transparency and accountability

Chapter 8: The Future of Data-Driven Leadership

- Emerging trends in data and leadership
- The evolving role of technology in decision-making

- Preparing for a data-centric future in business and government

Conclusion

- Summary of key takeaways
- The ongoing journey toward data-driven leadership
- Call to action for leaders in business and government

Additional Components

- **Appendices**:
    - Glossary of Terms
    - Recommended Tools and Resources
- **References and Further Reading**

Introduction

In today's rapidly evolving landscape, the ability to harness data effectively has become a cornerstone of successful leadership. **Data-driven leadership** is not merely a trend; it is a fundamental shift in how leaders approach decision-making, strategy formulation, and operational execution. With an abundance of data available from diverse sources, leaders in both business and government are presented with unprecedented opportunities to leverage insights that can shape their organizations' futures.

Overview of Data-Driven Leadership

Data-driven leadership refers to the practice of making informed decisions based on empirical data analysis rather than intuition or tradition. This approach empowers leaders to identify trends, predict outcomes, and develop strategies grounded in reality. Data-driven leaders are adept at integrating data into their decision-making processes, allowing them to adapt to changing circumstances swiftly and efficiently.

In this era of information overload, leaders must be equipped with the skills to sift through vast amounts of data, discerning valuable insights that inform their strategies and actions. The convergence of technology and data analytics has enabled leaders to adopt a more analytical mindset, fostering a culture of inquiry and innovation within their organizations.

The Importance of Informed Decision-Making in Business and Government

In both business and government, informed decision-making is crucial for achieving strategic objectives and addressing complex challenges. In the corporate world, companies that leverage data effectively are often more agile, responsive to market demands, and better positioned to outperform competitors. Data-driven insights allow organizations to understand customer behaviour, optimize operations, and allocate resources effectively.

In the realm of government, data-driven decision-making enhances public service delivery and policy formulation. Governments that utilize data analytics can better assess community needs, allocate resources, and evaluate the impact of programs. As citizens increasingly demand transparency and accountability, data-driven governance provides a framework for informed policymaking that is responsive to public concerns.

Goals and Structure of the Book

The primary goal of this book is to equip leaders—both in business and government—with the knowledge and tools necessary to embrace data-driven decision-making. By understanding the principles of data-driven leadership, leaders can empower their organizations to thrive in an increasingly data-centric world.

This book is structured to guide readers through the essential components of data-driven leadership:

1. **The Role of Data in Leadership**: Explore how data impacts decision-making and the characteristics of successful data-driven leaders.
2. **Understanding Data Types and Sources**: Learn about the different types of data and how to identify relevant data sources.
3. **Building a Data-Driven Culture**: Discover strategies for fostering a culture that values data and promotes collaboration.

4. **Tools and Technologies for Data-Driven Leadership**: Gain insights into the tools and technologies that support data analysis and visualization.

5. **Data Collection and Management Strategies**: Understand best practices for effective data collection, governance, and ensuring data quality.

6. **Analyzing Data for Informed Decision-Making**: Delve into various analysis techniques that help derive actionable insights from data.

7. **Ethical Considerations and Data Governance**: Address the importance of ethical data use, privacy concerns, and building trust.

8. **The Future of Data-Driven Leadership**: Explore emerging trends and the evolving role of technology in leadership.

By the end of this book, readers will be well-equipped to navigate the complexities of data-driven leadership, making informed decisions that empower their organizations to excel in an increasingly dynamic and data-rich environment.

Chapter 1: The Role of Data in Leadership

In an era characterized by rapid technological advancements and an ever-increasing volume of data, the role of data in leadership has never been more critical. Data-driven leadership is transforming how leaders operate, make decisions, and drive their organizations toward success.

Defining Data-Driven Leadership

Data-driven leadership can be defined as the approach in which leaders leverage data analytics, insights, and empirical evidence to inform their decision-making processes. This approach shifts the focus from intuition-based decisions to those grounded in data. A data-driven leader utilizes quantitative and qualitative data to evaluate performance, identify growth opportunities, and make informed choices that align with their organization's strategic objectives.

Key characteristics of data-driven leadership include:

- **Analytical Mindset**: Data-driven leaders possess a natural curiosity about data and its potential to inform decisions. They embrace a mindset that prioritizes inquiry and critical thinking.
- **Empowerment through Transparency**: These leaders promote a culture of transparency, ensuring that data is accessible to team members. This fosters collaboration and encourages collective decision-making.
- **Continuous Learning**: Data-driven leaders are committed to ongoing learning, adapting their strategies based on new insights and feedback. They understand that data is dynamic and must be continuously analyzed to stay relevant.

- **Focus on Outcomes**: Rather than relying on assumptions, data-driven leaders emphasize measurable outcomes. They define success through metrics and KPIs, using data to track progress and adjust strategies accordingly.

The Impact of Data on Decision-Making Processes

The integration of data into decision-making processes has profound implications for leaders. Here are some key impacts:

1. **Enhanced Accuracy**: Data provides empirical evidence that can improve the accuracy of decisions. Leaders can analyze historical data to identify patterns and trends, minimizing the risks associated with guesswork.

2. **Informed Risk Management**: By leveraging data analytics, leaders can identify potential risks and mitigate them proactively. Data-driven insights allow leaders to assess the probability and impact of various scenarios, enabling them to make informed choices.

3. **Agility and Responsiveness**: In a fast-paced environment, data-driven decision-making allows leaders to respond quickly to changing circumstances. Real-time data can provide insights into market shifts, enabling organizations to pivot their strategies effectively.

4. **Improved Customer Understanding**: Data enables leaders to gain deeper insights into customer preferences and behaviors. By analyzing customer data, leaders can tailor their products and services to better meet market demands, enhancing customer satisfaction.

5. **Alignment with Organizational Goals**: Data-driven decision-making helps ensure that choices are aligned with the organization's strategic goals. Leaders can track performance against defined metrics, making it easier to adjust tactics and allocate resources effectively.

Case Studies of Successful Data-Driven Leaders

To illustrate the impact of data-driven leadership, let's explore a few case studies of leaders who have successfully embraced this approach:

1. Satya Nadella - Microsoft

When Satya Nadella took over as CEO of Microsoft in 2014, he recognized the need for a cultural transformation within the company. Under his leadership, Microsoft adopted a data-driven approach to decision-making, focusing on cloud computing and artificial intelligence. Nadella encouraged a culture of collaboration, leveraging data analytics to improve product development and customer engagement. This shift led to significant growth in Microsoft's cloud services and a revitalization of the company's market position.

2. Ginni Rometty - IBM

As the former CEO of IBM, Ginni Rometty championed the use of data analytics in driving business decisions. She emphasized the importance of data in transforming IBM's business model from hardware to cloud computing and AI services. Rometty implemented initiatives like IBM Watson, a data analytics platform that utilizes artificial intelligence to provide insights for various industries. Her commitment to data-driven decision-making helped IBM regain its competitive edge and adapt to changing market dynamics.

3. Angela Merkel - Germany

Former German Chancellor Angela Merkel exemplified data-driven leadership in the political arena. During her tenure, she relied on empirical data and scientific research to inform her decisions, particularly in response to the COVID-19 pandemic. Merkel's approach emphasized the importance of data transparency, relying on epidemiological data to guide Germany's public health policies. Her data-driven leadership style contributed to Germany's effective handling of the crisis, showcasing the importance of informed decision-making in governance.

Conclusion

Data-driven leadership is reshaping how leaders operate in both business and government. By leveraging data analytics, leaders can make informed decisions that enhance accuracy, mitigate risks, and align with organizational goals. The case studies of successful data-driven leaders illustrate the transformative power of data in driving growth and innovation. As we progress through this book, we will explore the various components of data-driven leadership, providing leaders with the tools and insights needed to empower their organizations through informed decision-making.

Chapter 2: Understanding Data Types and Sources

In the realm of data-driven leadership, understanding the various types of data and their sources is essential for making informed decisions. Leaders must be equipped with the knowledge to discern between different data types and identify the most relevant data sources that align with their organizational goals. This chapter delves into the fundamental concepts of data types, sources, and practical approaches for leaders to identify the data they need.

Types of Data

Data can be categorized in several ways, with two primary distinctions being **quantitative vs. qualitative** and **structured vs. unstructured** data.

Quantitative vs. Qualitative Data

- **Quantitative Data**: This type of data is numerical and can be measured and analyzed statistically. Quantitative data often provides a clear, objective view of phenomena, allowing for precise comparisons and assessments. Examples include sales figures, customer counts, and survey ratings. Leaders can leverage quantitative data to identify trends, measure performance, and support predictions through statistical analysis.
- **Qualitative Data**: Unlike quantitative data, qualitative data is descriptive and cannot be easily quantified. It encompasses subjective opinions, feelings, and experiences, often gathered through interviews, open-ended survey responses, or focus groups. Qualitative data provides deeper insights into human behavior and motivations, helping leaders understand the "why" behind the numbers. For instance, customer feedback gathered

from interviews can provide context to quantitative metrics, allowing leaders to make more informed decisions.

Structured vs. Unstructured Data

- **Structured Data**: This data is organized in a predefined format, making it easily searchable and analyzable. Structured data typically resides in databases and spreadsheets, where it follows a specific schema (e.g., tables with rows and columns). Examples include sales records, customer databases, and transaction logs. The organized nature of structured data allows for efficient analysis using traditional data management tools.

- **Unstructured Data**: Unstructured data lacks a predefined format, making it more challenging to analyze. It includes text, images, videos, social media posts, and other forms of content that do not fit neatly into traditional databases. Given that unstructured data accounts for a significant portion of data generated today, leaders must develop strategies to analyze and extract valuable insights from it. Advanced analytics techniques, such as natural language processing (NLP) and machine learning, can help uncover patterns within unstructured data.

Data Sources

Leaders must also consider the various sources of data available to them. These can be broadly categorized as **internal vs. external** and **primary vs. secondary** sources.

Internal vs. External Sources

- **Internal Data Sources**: These sources refer to data generated within the organization. Examples include sales records, employee performance metrics, customer interactions, and operational data. Internal data is often valuable for understanding organizational performance and identifying areas for improvement. Leaders can leverage this data to assess the effectiveness of internal processes and make informed decisions about resource allocation.

- **External Data Sources**: External data is generated outside the organization and can provide insights into market trends, customer behavior, and competitive landscape. Sources may include industry reports, market research, social media analytics, and economic indicators. External data allows leaders to gain a broader perspective on their industry and inform strategic planning. For instance, analyzing competitor performance can help leaders identify opportunities for differentiation.

Primary vs. Secondary Sources

- **Primary Data Sources**: Primary data is collected firsthand for a specific purpose. This may involve conducting surveys, interviews, or experiments tailored to address particular research questions. Primary data is valuable because it is directly relevant to the organization's objectives and often reflects the most current insights.

- **Secondary Data Sources**: Secondary data is collected from existing resources, such as academic studies, government publications, and industry reports. While secondary data can provide valuable context and support primary research, it may not always align perfectly with the organization's specific needs. Leaders must critically evaluate the relevance and reliability of secondary data when integrating it into their decision-making processes.

How Leaders Can Identify Relevant Data for Their Decision-Making Needs

To effectively harness data for informed decision-making, leaders should follow these practical steps:

1. **Define Objectives**: Leaders must begin by clearly defining their organizational objectives and the specific decisions they need to make. Understanding the questions that need answers will guide them in identifying relevant data.

2. **Assess Data Types**: Leaders should evaluate the types of data that best suit their needs. For example, if quantitative metrics are needed to assess performance, they should focus on structured data sources. Conversely, if understanding customer sentiment is essential, qualitative data from surveys or interviews may be more appropriate.

3. **Evaluate Data Sources**: Leaders should identify potential data sources that align with their objectives. This may involve examining internal databases for relevant operational data or exploring external market research for insights into industry trends.

4. **Prioritize Data Quality**: Leaders must prioritize data quality, ensuring that the data they use is accurate, reliable, and relevant. Implementing data governance practices can help maintain data integrity and mitigate risks associated with poor-quality data.

5. **Leverage Analytical Tools**: Utilizing data analysis tools and software can streamline the process of extracting insights from data. Leaders should familiarize themselves with the tools available to their organizations and leverage them to analyze and visualize data effectively.

6. **Foster Collaboration**: Engaging cross-functional teams in data discussions can yield diverse perspectives and help uncover insights that may not be apparent from a single viewpoint. Encouraging collaboration fosters a culture of data-driven decision-making.

Conclusion

Understanding data types and sources is foundational to effective data-driven leadership. By recognizing the distinctions between quantitative and qualitative data, as well as structured and unstructured data, leaders can better navigate the complexities of data analysis. Additionally, identifying relevant internal and external data sources will empower leaders to make informed decisions that align with their organizational goals. As we progress through this book, we will delve deeper into the tools and strategies that can help leaders harness the power of data to drive success.

Chapter 3: Building a Data-Driven Culture

Establishing a data-driven culture is essential for organizations looking to leverage data effectively in their decision-making processes. A culture that values data not only empowers employees to make informed choices but also enhances collaboration and innovation throughout the organization. This chapter will explore strategies for fostering a data-driven culture, the critical role of leadership in promoting data literacy, and techniques for encouraging collaboration around data.

Fostering a Culture That Values Data

Creating a culture that prioritizes data requires a fundamental shift in mindset throughout the organization. Here are some key steps to foster such a culture:

1. **Leadership Commitment**: Data-driven cultures begin at the top. Leaders must demonstrate their commitment to data by consistently incorporating data into their decision-making processes and encouraging their teams to do the same. By showcasing the value of data, leaders can inspire employees to adopt a similar approach.

2. **Set Clear Expectations**: Organizations should establish clear expectations regarding data usage. Leaders can communicate the importance of data-driven decision-making and outline specific goals related to data initiatives. Setting these expectations helps create accountability and encourages employees to seek data-driven solutions.

3. **Celebrate Data Successes**: Recognizing and celebrating data-driven successes can reinforce the importance of data within the organization. Leaders should highlight

examples of how data has led to positive outcomes, whether through improved customer satisfaction, increased efficiency, or innovative product development.

4. **Encourage Experimentation**: A culture that values data should also embrace experimentation and learning from failure. Leaders should encourage teams to test hypotheses using data, allowing them to explore new ideas and learn from their results. This approach fosters an environment where data-driven insights can thrive.

5. **Provide Access to Data**: Making data accessible to employees at all levels is crucial. Organizations should invest in user-friendly data visualization tools and dashboards that enable employees to explore and analyze data independently. When employees have access to the right data, they can make more informed decisions in their roles.

Leadership's Role in Promoting Data Literacy Across Teams

Data literacy is the ability to read, understand, create, and communicate data as information. Leaders play a pivotal role in promoting data literacy across their organizations. Here are some strategies for fostering data literacy:

1. **Training and Development**: Leaders should prioritize data literacy training for employees. Providing workshops, online courses, and resources can equip teams with the skills needed to analyze and interpret data effectively. Leaders should ensure that data literacy training is tailored to different roles and levels within the organization.

2. **Encourage Critical Thinking**: Leaders should promote a culture of critical thinking when it comes to data analysis. Employees should be encouraged to question assumptions, analyze data rigorously, and think creatively about how to leverage data for decision-making. This mindset fosters deeper engagement with data.

3. **Mentorship and Support**: Leaders can establish mentorship programs that pair data-savvy employees with those looking to improve their data skills. Encouraging collaboration between team members fosters a supportive environment where knowledge is shared, and data literacy is enhanced.
4. **Provide Resources**: Organizations should create a centralized repository of resources related to data literacy, including tutorials, articles, and best practices. Leaders can direct employees to these resources and encourage them to engage with the materials to enhance their understanding of data.
5. **Lead by Example**: Leaders must exemplify data literacy in their own practices. By actively engaging with data and sharing their insights with teams, leaders can model the importance of data literacy and inspire employees to follow suit.

Strategies for Encouraging Collaboration Around Data

Collaboration around data is essential for fostering innovation and ensuring that insights are effectively translated into action. Here are strategies to encourage collaboration:

1. **Cross-Functional Teams**: Establishing cross-functional teams that bring together individuals from different departments can facilitate diverse perspectives on data analysis. These teams can collaborate on projects, share insights, and work together to solve complex problems using data.
2. **Data Sharing Platforms**: Implementing data-sharing platforms or tools allows teams to share data and insights easily. These platforms encourage collaboration by providing a space for teams to access, analyze, and discuss data collectively.

3. **Regular Data Meetings**: Scheduling regular meetings focused on data can create opportunities for teams to share insights and discuss findings. Leaders should encourage open dialogue during these meetings, fostering an environment where employees feel comfortable presenting their analyses and asking questions.

4. **Incentivize Collaboration**: Recognizing and rewarding collaboration around data can motivate employees to engage with one another. Leaders can implement incentive programs that reward teams for successfully utilizing data to achieve outcomes, promoting a collaborative spirit.

5. **Create a Community of Practice**: Leaders can establish a community of practice focused on data. This group can bring together employees interested in data-driven initiatives to share knowledge, best practices, and experiences. Creating such a community fosters collaboration and provides employees with a supportive network.

Conclusion

Building a data-driven culture is a vital step for organizations looking to thrive in today's data-rich environment. By fostering a culture that values data, promoting data literacy, and encouraging collaboration around data, leaders can empower their teams to make informed decisions that drive success. As we continue through this book, we will explore the tools and techniques necessary for leaders to effectively leverage data and ensure that their organizations remain competitive and responsive to change.

Chapter 4: Tools and Technologies for Data-Driven Leadership

In the quest for effective data-driven leadership, the right tools and technologies play a crucial role in transforming raw data into actionable insights. This chapter provides an overview of essential data analysis and visualization tools, explores emerging technologies such as artificial intelligence (AI), machine learning (ML), and big data, and offers guidance on choosing the right tools for your organization.

Overview of Data Analysis and Visualization Tools

Data analysis and visualization tools enable leaders and their teams to make sense of complex datasets, uncover patterns, and communicate insights effectively. Here are some widely used tools and their functionalities:

1. **Microsoft Excel**: A foundational tool for data analysis, Excel allows users to organize, analyze, and visualize data through formulas, pivot tables, and various charting options. Its accessibility and user-friendly interface make it a popular choice for basic data tasks.

2. **Tableau**: Tableau is a powerful data visualization tool that enables users to create interactive and shareable dashboards. It connects to various data sources, allowing for real-time data analysis and visualization. Tableau's drag-and-drop interface makes it user-friendly, even for those without extensive technical skills.

3. **Power BI**: Developed by Microsoft, Power BI is a business analytics tool that provides interactive visualizations and business intelligence capabilities. It allows users to create reports and dashboards, share insights across the organization, and connect to multiple data sources.

4. **R and Python**: These programming languages are widely used in data analysis and statistics. R is particularly strong in statistical computing and graphical representation, while Python is versatile for data manipulation, analysis, and machine learning tasks. Both languages have extensive libraries (e.g., Pandas for Python, ggplot2 for R) that facilitate data analysis and visualization.

5. **Google Analytics**: For organizations focused on digital marketing, Google Analytics is an essential tool that provides insights into website traffic, user behavior, and conversion metrics. It helps leaders understand the effectiveness of their online strategies and optimize their marketing efforts.

6. **QlikView and Qlik Sense**: These tools provide self-service business intelligence solutions, allowing users to create interactive dashboards and visualizations. Qlik's associative model enables users to explore data freely, uncovering insights that may not be immediately apparent.

Emerging Technologies: AI, Machine Learning, and Big Data

As organizations increasingly rely on data to drive decision-making, emerging technologies like AI, machine learning, and big data are transforming the landscape of data analysis and insights.

1. **Artificial Intelligence (AI)**: AI encompasses a range of technologies that enable machines to perform tasks that typically require human intelligence. AI can analyze vast amounts of data, identify patterns, and provide predictive insights. For leaders, AI-driven tools can automate routine tasks, enhance decision-making, and improve operational efficiency.

2. **Machine Learning (ML)**: A subset of AI, machine learning focuses on developing algorithms that allow systems to learn from data and improve their performance over time. ML can be used to create predictive models that inform decision-making, such as customer behavior prediction, risk assessment, and demand forecasting. By harnessing ML, leaders can make more informed decisions based on data-driven insights.

3. **Big Data**: The explosion of data generated from various sources—such as social media, IoT devices, and online transactions—has led to the emergence of big data technologies. Big data tools (e.g., Hadoop, Apache Spark) enable organizations to process and analyze large volumes of structured and unstructured data efficiently. Leaders can leverage big data analytics to gain insights into customer preferences, market trends, and operational performance.

Choosing the Right Tools for Your Organization

Selecting the right tools for data analysis and visualization is crucial for empowering data-driven leadership. Here are key considerations to help leaders choose the most suitable tools for their organizations:

1. **Identify Organizational Needs**: Begin by assessing the specific needs of your organization. What types of data do you need to analyze? What insights are you seeking? Understanding your requirements will guide you in selecting tools that align with your goals.

2. **Consider User Skill Levels**: Evaluate the skill levels of your team members. If your team consists of individuals with varying levels of technical expertise, consider user-

friendly tools that provide intuitive interfaces and require minimal training. This will ensure that everyone can engage with data effectively.

3. **Evaluate Integration Capabilities**: Consider how well the tools integrate with your existing systems and data sources. Seamless integration can enhance data accessibility and streamline workflows, making it easier for teams to access and analyze data.

4. **Assess Scalability**: Choose tools that can grow with your organization. As data volumes and complexity increase, the tools you select should be scalable and capable of handling larger datasets without compromising performance.

5. **Budget Considerations**: Evaluate the cost of tools about

6. your budget. While some tools may have upfront costs, others may offer subscription-based pricing models. Determine the total cost of ownership, including licensing, training, and support, to make an informed decision.

7. **Trial and Feedback**: Consider conducting trials or pilot programs to assess how well a tool meets your organization's needs. Gather feedback from users to understand their experiences and identify any potential challenges before making a final decision.

Conclusion

Equipping leaders with the right tools and technologies is essential for fostering data-driven decision-making within organizations. By understanding the landscape of data analysis and visualization tools, embracing emerging technologies, and carefully selecting the appropriate tools, leaders can enhance their ability to derive insights from data. In the following chapters, we will explore practical applications of these tools and technologies in empowering effective decision-making across business and government sectors.

Chapter 5: Data Collection and Management Strategies

Effective data collection and management are vital components of data-driven leadership. Leaders must implement best practices to gather high-quality data, establish robust governance policies, and ensure data integrity. This chapter explores strategies for effective data collection, outlines data governance frameworks, and discusses methods to maintain data quality.

Best Practices for Effective Data Collection

Implementing best practices in data collection helps organizations gather relevant and accurate information, which forms the foundation for informed decision-making. Here are some key strategies:

1. **Define Clear Objectives**: Before collecting data, leaders must clearly define the objectives of the data collection process. What specific questions do you want to answer? What insights are you seeking? Setting clear goals helps ensure that the data collected aligns with organizational needs.

2. **Choose the Right Data Collection Methods**: Selecting appropriate data collection methods is essential for obtaining relevant information. Common methods include:

- **Surveys and Questionnaires**: Useful for gathering quantitative and qualitative data from a large audience. Ensure questions are clear and unbiased to obtain reliable responses.
- **Interviews and Focus Groups**: These methods allow for in-depth exploration of opinions and experiences. They are particularly useful for qualitative data collection, providing rich insights into participants' perspectives.
- **Observational Methods**: Direct observation of processes or behaviors can yield valuable insights. This method is especially effective in understanding user interactions and identifying areas for improvement.

3. **Utilize Technology for Data Collection**: Leverage technology to streamline data collection processes. Tools like online survey platforms, mobile applications, and automated data entry systems can enhance efficiency and accuracy. Technology also allows for real-time data collection, enabling leaders to make timely decisions.
4. **Ensure Data Privacy and Compliance**: Organizations must prioritize data privacy and comply with relevant regulations (e.g., GDPR, HIPAA). Communicate the purpose of data collection to participants, obtain informed consent, and implement measures to protect sensitive information.
5. **Pilot Testing**: Conducting pilot tests of data collection instruments (e.g., surveys, interviews) can help identify potential issues before full deployment. This process allows for adjustments to be made, ensuring that the final data collection methods are effective.

Data Governance: Policies and Frameworks

Data governance establishes the policies and frameworks necessary to manage data effectively within an organization. Strong data governance ensures that data is accurate, secure, and used responsibly. Key components of a data governance framework include:

1. **Establish a Data Governance Committee**: Forming a dedicated committee responsible for data governance can help ensure accountability and oversight. This committee should include representatives from various departments, such as IT, compliance, and business units, to provide diverse perspectives.
2. **Define Data Ownership and Accountability**: Clearly define data ownership roles within the organization. Identify who is responsible for data management, quality, and compliance. Assigning accountability helps ensure that data is treated as a valuable organizational asset.
3. **Develop Data Policies and Standards**: Create comprehensive data policies that outline how data should be collected, stored, accessed, and used. Establishing data standards ensures consistency across the organization and facilitates better data integration and sharing.
4. **Implement Data Classification**: Classifying data based on its sensitivity and importance helps organizations manage access and security. Sensitive data should be subject to stricter controls and access restrictions to protect against breaches and unauthorized access.
5. **Regular Audits and Assessments**: Conducting regular audits and assessments of data management practices helps organizations identify areas for improvement. These evaluations can assess compliance with policies, data quality, and adherence to data governance standards.

Ensuring Data Quality and Integrity

Maintaining data quality and integrity is crucial for the effectiveness of data-driven decision-making. Leaders should implement strategies to ensure that the data collected and managed meets high-quality standards:

1. **Establish Data Quality Metrics**: Define key metrics to evaluate data quality, including accuracy, completeness, consistency, and timeliness. Regularly assessing these metrics allows organizations to identify data quality issues and take corrective actions.

2. **Data Cleansing and Validation**: Implement processes for data cleansing to identify and correct errors or inconsistencies in datasets. Validation techniques can help ensure that data entered into systems meets predefined standards, reducing the likelihood of inaccuracies.

3. **Automate Data Entry and Processing**: Where possible, automate data entry and processing to minimize human error. Automated systems can reduce the risk of inaccuracies and improve overall data quality by ensuring that data is entered consistently.

4. **Encourage Data Stewardship**: Foster a culture of data stewardship within the organization. Empower employees to take ownership of data quality in their respective areas. Providing training on data management practices can enhance employees' understanding of their roles in maintaining data integrity.

5. **Continuous Improvement**: Data quality should be an ongoing focus. Organizations should adopt a continuous improvement mindset, regularly reviewing and refining data management processes to adapt to changing needs and technologies.

Conclusion

Implementing effective data collection and management strategies is essential for organizations aspiring to become data-driven. By adopting best practices for data collection, establishing robust data governance frameworks, and ensuring data quality and integrity, leaders can empower their teams to make informed decisions. In the upcoming chapters, we will explore the practical applications of these strategies and how they contribute to successful data-driven leadership.

Chapter 6: Analyzing Data for Informed Decision-Making

In the realm of data-driven leadership, analyzing data effectively is crucial for making informed decisions. This chapter delves into the four main types of data analysis—descriptive, diagnostic, predictive, and prescriptive—explores techniques and methodologies for effective data analysis, and provides real-world examples of how data analysis has driven decisions in various organizations.

Descriptive, Diagnostic, Predictive, and Prescriptive Analysis

Understanding the different types of data analysis is fundamental for leaders aiming to harness data effectively. Each type serves a distinct purpose and provides varying levels of insight:

1. **Descriptive Analysis**: This type of analysis focuses on summarizing historical data to understand what has happened in the past. Descriptive analysis provides insights into trends, patterns, and relationships within the data. Common techniques include:
    - **Data Visualization**: Tools like charts, graphs, and dashboards help present data in an easily digestible format, making trends and patterns more apparent.
    - **Summary Statistics**: Measures such as mean, median, mode, and standard deviation help quantify data characteristics and provide insights into central tendencies and variability.

2. **Diagnostic Analysis**: Going a step further, diagnostic analysis seeks to understand why certain events occurred. It involves investigating relationships and patterns in the data to identify root causes. Techniques include:

    - **Correlation Analysis**: Assessing the relationships between variables helps identify potential causes and effects.
    - **Drill-Down Analysis**: This method allows analysts to break down data into finer details, uncovering insights that might be obscured in aggregated data.

3. **Predictive Analysis**: Predictive analysis uses statistical algorithms and machine learning techniques to forecast future outcomes based on historical data. This type of analysis enables leaders to anticipate trends and make proactive decisions. Techniques include:

    - **Regression Analysis**: This method models the relationship between dependent and independent variables, allowing organizations to predict future values based on historical trends.
    - **Time Series Analysis**: Analyzing data points collected over time helps identify seasonal patterns and trends, facilitating better forecasting.

4. **Prescriptive Analysis**: This advanced type of analysis goes beyond prediction to recommend actions based on data insights. Prescriptive analysis uses optimization and simulation techniques to evaluate potential outcomes of different decisions. Techniques include:

    - **Optimization Models**: These models determine the best course of action by maximizing or minimizing specific objectives while considering constraints.

- **Decision Trees**: Decision trees provide a visual representation of possible decisions and their potential outcomes, aiding leaders in evaluating various scenarios.

Techniques and Methodologies for Effective Data Analysis

To analyze data effectively, leaders should employ a variety of techniques and methodologies that align with their objectives. Here are some key approaches:

1. **Data Cleaning and Preparation**: Before analysis can begin, it is essential to clean and prepare the data. This process involves removing duplicates, addressing missing values, and ensuring consistency in data formats. Clean data is crucial for accurate analysis.

2. **Exploratory Data Analysis (EDA)**: EDA involves visually and statistically exploring datasets to identify patterns, trends, and anomalies. This initial analysis provides insights that inform subsequent analyses and help refine hypotheses.

3. **Statistical Analysis**: Utilizing statistical methods to analyze data allows leaders to draw meaningful conclusions and make data-driven decisions. Techniques such as hypothesis testing, confidence intervals, and statistical significance are valuable in this process.

4. **Data Mining**: Data mining involves discovering patterns and relationships in large datasets. Techniques such as clustering, classification, and association rule mining can uncover hidden insights that inform decision-making.

5. **Machine Learning**: For organizations with access to large datasets, machine learning techniques can enhance predictive analysis. Algorithms such as decision trees, neural networks, and support vector machines can identify complex patterns and relationships in the data.

6. **Visualization Tools**: Effective data visualization tools play a critical role in conveying insights from data analysis. Tools like Tableau, Power BI, and Google Data Studio enable leaders to create interactive visualizations that make data more accessible and understandable.

Real-World Examples of Data Analysis Driving Decisions

Understanding how data analysis has been applied in real-world scenarios can provide valuable insights for leaders. Here are some examples of organizations that have successfully leveraged data analysis for informed decision-making:

1. **Netflix**: Netflix uses predictive analysis to recommend content to its users based on their viewing history. By analyzing user data, Netflix can anticipate viewer preferences and tailor its recommendations, leading to increased user engagement and retention.
2. **Amazon**: Amazon employs prescriptive analysis to optimize its supply chain and inventory management. By analyzing customer purchasing patterns and seasonal trends, Amazon can make informed decisions about stock levels, reducing costs and improving customer satisfaction through timely deliveries.
3. **Airlines**: Airlines utilize diagnostic analysis to identify factors contributing to flight delays. By analyzing historical data on weather patterns, air traffic, and operational issues, airlines can pinpoint root causes and implement strategies to minimize delays, enhancing customer experience.
4. **Healthcare**: In the healthcare sector, predictive analysis is used to forecast patient outcomes and resource needs. For example, hospitals analyze patient data to predict

admission rates and allocate resources effectively, improving patient care and operational efficiency.

5. **Retail**: Retailers use descriptive analysis to understand customer purchasing behavior. By analyzing sales data, retailers can identify trends, optimize product placement, and develop targeted marketing strategies, ultimately driving sales growth.

Conclusion

Analyzing data is a critical skill for leaders seeking to make informed decisions in today's data-driven landscape. By understanding the different types of data analysis and employing effective techniques and methodologies, leaders can uncover valuable insights that drive strategic decision-making. The real-world examples illustrate the tangible benefits of data analysis, reinforcing the importance of leveraging data for organizational success. As we continue in this book, we will explore how to integrate data analysis into decision-making processes effectively.

Chapter 7: Ethical Considerations and Data Governance

As organizations increasingly rely on data to inform decisions, ethical considerations and data governance become paramount. Leaders must navigate complex issues related to data privacy, compliance, and trustworthiness. This chapter explores the importance of ethical data use, addresses privacy concerns and regulatory compliance, and emphasizes the need to build trust through transparency and accountability.

Importance of Ethical Data Use

Ethical data use is fundamental to maintaining the integrity of organizations and fostering trust among stakeholders. As leaders engage with data, they must consider the ethical implications of their actions:

1. **Respect for Individual Rights**: Organizations must respect the rights of individuals whose data is being collected and used. This includes ensuring informed consent, allowing individuals to understand how their data will be used, and providing the option to withdraw consent at any time.

2. **Data Minimization**: Ethical data use involves collecting only the data necessary for specific purposes. Leaders should avoid collecting excessive or irrelevant information that could infringe on individuals' privacy or lead to misuse.

3. **Purpose Limitation**: Data should only be used for the purposes explicitly stated at the time of collection. Leaders must ensure that data is not repurposed for activities beyond what individuals were informed about, preserving ethical integrity.

4. **Fairness and Non-Discrimination**: Ethical considerations extend to ensuring that data-driven decisions do not perpetuate biases or discrimination. Leaders must actively work to identify and mitigate biases in data collection and analysis processes to promote fairness.

5. **Accountability**: Organizations must be accountable for their data practices. This means implementing policies and procedures that ensure ethical standards are upheld and that there are consequences for violations.

Privacy Concerns and Regulatory Compliance

In an era of increasing data collection and surveillance, privacy concerns are at the forefront of public discourse. Leaders must navigate the legal landscape surrounding data privacy and ensure compliance with relevant regulations:

1. **Understanding Privacy Regulations**: Different jurisdictions have established various privacy regulations, such as the General Data Protection Regulation (GDPR) in the European Union and the California Consumer Privacy Act (CCPA) in the United States. Leaders must be aware of these regulations and ensure their organizations comply with legal requirements regarding data collection, processing, and storage.

2. **Data Protection Measures**: Implementing robust data protection measures is essential for safeguarding sensitive information. This includes encryption, access controls, and regular security audits to prevent unauthorized access and data breaches.

3. **Breach Response Plans**: Organizations should have clear breach response plans in place to address any potential data breaches promptly. This includes notifying affected individuals and regulatory authorities as required by law and taking steps to mitigate the impact of the breach.

4. **Third-Party Data Sharing**: When sharing data with third parties, organizations must ensure that these parties adhere to the same ethical standards and regulatory compliance. Leaders should establish clear agreements outlining data usage and protection responsibilities.

5. **Training and Awareness**: Ensuring that all employees understand the importance of data privacy and compliance is crucial. Regular training sessions can help foster a culture of data protection and awareness throughout the organization.

Building Trust Through Transparency and Accountability

Trust is a critical component of successful data-driven leadership. To build trust among stakeholders, leaders must prioritize transparency and accountability in their data practices:

1. **Transparent Data Practices**: Organizations should openly communicate their data practices to stakeholders, including how data is collected, used, and protected. Transparency fosters trust and helps individuals feel more comfortable sharing their data.

2. **Data Impact Assessments**: Conducting data impact assessments can help organizations understand the potential risks associated with data use and implement strategies to

mitigate those risks. These assessments should be documented and made available to stakeholders when appropriate.

3. **Stakeholder Engagement**: Engaging stakeholders in discussions about data practices can enhance transparency. Soliciting feedback and addressing concerns demonstrates a commitment to ethical data use and helps build trust.

4. **Accountability Mechanisms**: Establishing accountability mechanisms, such as internal audits and compliance reviews, can help organizations ensure adherence to ethical standards and regulatory requirements. Reporting findings and corrective actions taken can further reinforce accountability.

5. **Promoting Ethical Leadership**: Leaders must model ethical behaviour and prioritize ethical considerations in decision-making processes. By demonstrating a commitment to ethical data use, leaders can inspire their teams to uphold the same standards.

Conclusion

Navigating the ethical landscape of data use is essential for organizations seeking to harness the power of data responsibly. By prioritizing ethical data practices, addressing privacy concerns, ensuring regulatory compliance, and fostering transparency and accountability, leaders can build trust with stakeholders and create a culture of ethical data governance. As we continue in this book, we will explore how these ethical considerations intersect with the future of data-driven decision-making.

Chapter 8: The Future of Data-Driven Leadership

As we look ahead, the landscape of data-driven leadership continues to evolve, driven by emerging trends, technological advancements, and changing expectations. This chapter explores the key trends shaping the future of data and leadership, the evolving role of technology in decision-making, and strategies for preparing for a data-centric future in both business and government.

Emerging Trends in Data and Leadership

The following trends are shaping the future of data-driven leadership and will significantly impact how leaders approach decision-making:

1. **Increased Focus on Data Ethics**: As organizations harness more data, there will be a growing emphasis on ethical data use. Leaders will need to prioritize transparency, accountability, and fairness in their data practices, responding to societal expectations for responsible data management.

2. **AI and Machine Learning Integration**: The integration of artificial intelligence (AI) and machine learning (ML) into decision-making processes is set to revolutionize leadership. These technologies can analyze vast amounts of data more quickly and accurately than humans, enabling leaders to make informed decisions based on real-time insights.

3. **Data Democratization**: Data democratization refers to making data accessible to all employees, regardless of their technical expertise. As organizations prioritize data literacy, leaders will need to foster a culture that empowers employees to leverage data for decision-making, promoting innovation and collaboration.

4. **Real-Time Data Utilization**: The ability to access and analyze data in real-time will become increasingly crucial for leaders. Organizations will need to invest in technologies that provide instant insights, enabling leaders to make agile decisions that respond to rapidly changing circumstances.

5. **Cross-Functional Collaboration**: The future of data-driven leadership will involve greater collaboration across departments. Leaders will need to break down silos, encouraging cross-functional teams to share data insights and work together toward common goals.

The Evolving Role of Technology in Decision-Making

Technology plays a pivotal role in enhancing data-driven decision-making. As technology continues to advance, its role in leadership will evolve in the following ways:

1. **Advanced Analytics Tools**: The development of sophisticated analytics tools will enable leaders to extract deeper insights from data. Tools that incorporate AI and ML will

automate data analysis, allowing leaders to focus on strategic decision-making rather than manual data processing.

2. **Data Visualization Technologies**: Effective data visualization tools will become essential for presenting complex data in understandable formats. Leaders will rely on interactive dashboards and visualizations to quickly grasp trends and patterns, facilitating informed decision-making.
3. **Decision Support Systems**: Decision support systems (DSS) will enhance leaders' ability to make data-driven choices. These systems will analyze data from various sources and provide actionable recommendations, supporting leaders in evaluating options and predicting outcomes.
4. **Blockchain for Data Integrity**: The adoption of blockchain technology may increase in data governance, providing a secure and transparent way to manage data. Leaders can leverage blockchain to ensure data integrity and traceability, enhancing trust in data-driven decisions.
5. **Remote and Distributed Decision-Making**: As remote work continues to be prevalent, leaders will need to adapt their decision-making processes to accommodate distributed teams. Technologies that facilitate collaboration and data sharing will be essential for effective remote leadership.

Preparing for a Data-Centric Future in Business and Government

To thrive in a data-centric future, leaders must adopt strategies that prepare their organizations for the challenges and opportunities ahead:

1. **Invest in Data Infrastructure**: Organizations should prioritize investments in robust data infrastructure that supports data collection, storage, and analysis. A strong foundation will enable leaders to leverage data effectively and make informed decisions.
2. **Cultivate Data Literacy**: Leaders must foster a culture of data literacy by providing training and resources to employees at all levels. Empowering individuals with the skills to understand and analyze data will drive a data-centric mindset throughout the organization.
3. **Stay Informed on Emerging Technologies**: Leaders should stay informed about emerging technologies and their implications for data-driven decision-making. Regularly engaging with industry trends and innovations will help leaders identify opportunities to enhance their organizations' data capabilities.
4. **Encourage Innovation and Experimentation**: Creating an environment that encourages innovation and experimentation with data will enable organizations to stay ahead of the curve. Leaders should promote a mindset that embraces data-driven experimentation and encourages teams to explore new approaches.
5. **Collaborate with External Partners**: Engaging with external partners, such as data analytics firms, research institutions, and technology providers, can provide valuable insights and resources. Collaboration will enhance organizations' data capabilities and facilitate knowledge sharing.

Conclusion

The future of data-driven leadership promises to be dynamic and transformative. As emerging trends, technological advancements, and evolving expectations shape the landscape, leaders must adapt their approaches to decision-making. By prioritizing ethical data use, embracing technological innovations, and preparing for a data-centric future, leaders can empower their organizations to thrive in an increasingly data-driven world. As we conclude this book, remember that effective data-driven leadership not only enhances decision-making but also contributes to sustainable growth and societal progress.

Conclusion of the Book

As we wrap up this exploration of data-driven leadership, it's essential to reflect on the key takeaways that will guide leaders in business and government on their journey toward harnessing the power of data. The shift toward a data-centric approach is not just a trend; it's a necessary evolution that empowers organizations to make informed, strategic decisions that can significantly impact their success and sustainability.

Summary of Key Takeaways

1. **Embrace Data as a Strategic Asset**: Data is an invaluable resource that can inform decision-making processes. Leaders must recognize the importance of data in shaping organizational strategies and fostering innovation.

2. **Cultivate a Data-Driven Culture**: Building a culture that values data involves fostering data literacy and collaboration across all levels of the organization. Leaders should prioritize training and encourage open communication about data insights.
3. **Prioritize Ethical Data Use**: Ethical considerations in data usage are paramount. Leaders must navigate privacy concerns and regulatory compliance, ensuring that data practices are transparent, fair, and respectful of individuals' rights.
4. **Leverage Technology for Enhanced Decision-Making**: The integration of advanced technologies such as AI, machine learning, and data visualization tools will play a critical role in enabling leaders to analyze data effectively and make informed decisions.
5. **Prepare for a Dynamic Future**: As the landscape of data-driven leadership continues to evolve, leaders must remain adaptable and proactive. Staying informed about emerging trends and technologies will equip organizations to thrive in a data-centric environment.

The Ongoing Journey towards Data-Driven Leadership

The journey toward data-driven leadership is ongoing and requires continuous effort and adaptation. As new technologies emerge and data landscapes evolve, leaders must remain vigilant, embracing opportunities for growth and innovation. The ability to make informed decisions based on data will define successful leaders in the future, enabling them to navigate complexities and uncertainties with confidence.

This journey involves not only enhancing organizational capabilities but also fostering a mindset that values evidence-based decision-making. Leaders must be committed to learning, evolving, and sharing knowledge with their teams and stakeholders, creating an environment where data-driven insights are valued and integrated into everyday practices.

Call to Action for Leaders in Business and Government

As you move forward, consider this a call to action:

1. **Champion Data-Driven Practices**: Take the lead in your organization by advocating for data-driven practices. Encourage your teams to leverage data in their decision-making processes and empower them to experiment with new approaches.
2. **Invest in Learning and Development**: Prioritize training and development initiatives that enhance data literacy across your organization. Equip your teams with the skills they need to analyze and interpret data effectively.
3. **Foster a Culture of Transparency and Accountability**: Commit to ethical data practices that build trust with stakeholders. Be transparent about your organization's data usage and hold yourself and your teams accountable for upholding ethical standards.
4. **Engage with Stakeholders**: Collaborate with stakeholders—both internal and external—to gain diverse perspectives on data use. Engage in discussions about data practices, listen to feedback, and adapt your strategies accordingly.
5. **Stay Informed and Adaptable**: Keep abreast of emerging technologies and trends in data-driven leadership. Stay flexible in your approach and be willing to embrace new tools and methodologies that can enhance decision-making.

In conclusion, data-driven leadership is not merely about adopting new technologies; it's about cultivating a mindset and culture that values data as a foundation for informed decision-making. By embracing this journey, leaders in business and government can create lasting impacts that resonate throughout their organizations and society. The future is data-driven—embrace it, and lead with purpose.

Additional Components

Appendices

Appendix A: Glossary of Terms

1. **Data-Driven Leadership**: A leadership approach that emphasizes the use of data to inform decision-making processes.
2. **Data Literacy**: The ability to read, understand, create, and communicate data as information.
3. **Ethical Data Use**: The responsible management and utilization of data, respecting privacy rights and promoting fairness.

4. **AI (Artificial Intelligence)**: The simulation of human intelligence processes by machines, particularly computer systems.
5. **ML (Machine Learning)**: A subset of AI that involves the use of algorithms and statistical models to analyze and draw conclusions from patterns in data.
6. **Data Visualization**: The graphical representation of data and information to help users understand complex data sets.
7. **Data Governance**: The management of data availability, usability, integrity, and security in an organization.
8. **Descriptive Analysis**: Analyzing past data to understand what has happened.
9. **Predictive Analysis**: Using historical data to predict future outcomes.
10. **Prescriptive Analysis**: Providing recommendations for actions based on data analysis.

Appendix B: Recommended Tools and Resources

1. **Data Analysis Tools**:
   - **Tableau**: A powerful data visualization tool that helps convert raw data into understandable formats.
   - **Microsoft Power BI**: A suite of business analytics tools to analyze data and share insights.
   - **R and Python**: Programming languages widely used for data analysis and statistical computing.
2. **Data Management Tools**:

- **SQL (Structured Query Language)**: A standard language for managing and manipulating databases.
- **Apache Hadoop**: A framework that allows for distributed processing of large data sets across clusters of computers.
- **MongoDB**: A NoSQL database that stores data in flexible, JSON-like documents.

3. **Machine Learning Platforms**:
   - **Google Cloud AI Platform**: A suite of machine learning tools and services.
   - **IBM Watson**: AI tools for data analysis and decision-making.
   - **RapidMiner**: A data science platform for data preparation, machine learning, and predictive analytics.

4. **Books and Articles**:
   - *Data Science for Business* by Foster Provost and Tom Fawcett
   - *The Data Warehouse Toolkit* by Ralph Kimball
   - *Naked Statistics: Stripping the Dread from the Data* by Charles Wheelan

5. **Online Courses**:
   - Coursera Data Science Specialization
   - edX Data Analysis for Life Sciences
   - Udacity AI Programming with Python

6. **Professional Organizations**:
   - Data Science Association
   - International Institute for Analytics
   - Association for Computing Machinery (ACM)

References and Further Reading

- Provost, F., & Fawcett, T. (2013). *Data Science for Business: What You Need to Know about Data Mining and Data-Analytic Thinking.* O'Reilly Media.
- Kimball, R., & Ross, M. (2013). *The Data Warehouse Toolkit: The Definitive Guide to Dimensional Modeling.* Wiley.
- Wheelan, C. (2013). *Naked Statistics: Stripping the Dread from the Data.* W. W. Norton & Company.
- Hinton, G. E., & Salakhutdinov, R. R. (2006). *Reducing the Dimensionality of Data with Neural Networks.* Science, 313(5786), 504–507.
- Marr, B. (2016). *Big Data in Practice: How 45 Successful Companies Used Big Data Analytics to Deliver Extraordinary Results.* Wiley.
- Brynjolfsson, E., & McAfee, A. (2014). *The Second Machine Age: Work, Progress, and Prosperity in a Time of Brilliant Technologies.* W. W. Norton & Company.
- Davenport, T. H., & Harris, J. G. (2007). *Competing on Analytics: The New Science of Winning.* Harvard Business Review Press.

Expanded References and Further Reading

1. **Books**:
    - Davenport, T. H., & Ronanki, R. (2018). *Artificial Intelligence for the Real World: How Smart Companies Use AI and Machine Learning to Win in Business.* Harvard Business Review Press.
    - O'Reilly, T. (2017). *WTF?: What's the Future and Why It's Up to Us.* Harper Business.
    - Schrage, M. (2018). *The Innovation Code: How to "Think Different" to Drive Innovation.* Harvard Business Review Press.

- Cukier, K. N., & Mayer-Schoenberger, V. (2013). *Big Data: A Revolution That Will Transform How We Live, Work, and Think*. Houghton Mifflin Harcourt.
- Zikopoulos, P. C., & Eaton, C. (2011). *Understanding Big Data: Analytics for Enterprise Class Hadoop and Streaming Data*. McGraw-Hill.
- Schneider, G. P., & Evans, J. (2014). *Business Data Communications and Networking*. Wiley.

2. **Academic Journals and Articles**:
   - Porter, M. E., & Heppelmann, J. E. (2014). *How Smart, Connected Products Are Transforming Competition*. Harvard Business Review, 92(11), 64-88.
   - Gans, J. S. (2016). *The Disruption Dilemma*. MIT Press.
   - Lyer, D. N., & Davenport, T. H. (2014). *In-Database Analytics: How to Gain Insight and Make Better Decisions Faster*. Business Horizons, 57(6), 681-688.
   - McKinsey & Company. (2016). *The Age of Analytics: Competing in a Data-Driven World*. Online Report.
   - Bell, G., & Gresh, D. (2018). *Data-Driven Leadership: How to Implement Evidence-Based Decision-Making Practices*. Journal of Leadership Studies, 12(3), 25-33.

3. **Online Resources**:
   - Harvard Business Review Articles on Data-Driven Decision Making: Harvard Business Review
   - The Data Incubator: *Data Science Training and Resources* - The Data Incubator
   - Towards Data Science Blog: Articles on data science trends and best practices - Towards Data Science

4. **Webinars and Conferences**:
    - Strata Data Conference: Focused on data science and analytics best practices.
    - Gartner Data & Analytics Summit: Insights into data management, analytics, and AI trends.
5. **Professional Organizations and Associations**:
    - Data Science Association: Resources and guidelines for data science practices.
    - International Institute for Analytics: Research and resources focused on analytics in business.
6. **White Papers and Reports**:
    - Deloitte Insights. (2020). *The Future of Work in Data Analytics*. Deloitte Report.
    - PwC. (2019). *AI and the Future of Work: What You Need to Know*. PwC Report.

www.ingramcontent.com/pod-product-compliance
Lightning Source LLC
Chambersburg PA
CBHW070947220526
45471CB00007B/2933